Roadmap

A CHOREOPOEM BY
MONICA PRINCE

sfwp.com

Library of Congress Cataloging-in-Publication Data
Names: Prince, Monica, author.
Title: Roadmap / a choreopoem by Monica Prince.
Description: Santa Fe, NM : SFWP, [2023] | Summary: "In this radical 21st century choreopoem, Dorian, a young American Black man, is tasked by an ancestral spirit to thwart his inevitable murder. He traces his family tree, from his grandmother to his offspring, uncovering secrets of sex work, self-harm, and assault alongside snapshots of BlackBoyJoy. Guided by The Novelist, an omniscient muse, and her troupe of dancers, Dorian must interrogate his legacy, forgive his past, and reckon with being Black in modern America. He tries on different selves and possible futures in his increasing desperation to experience the luxury of growing old and finding solace despite institutional racism declaring him a threat. Through the poetry, dance, and song of Roadmap, will Dorian overcome the odds or become another hashtag?"
—Provided by publisher.
Identifiers: LCCN 2022023971 (print) | LCCN 2022023972 (ebook) | ISBN 9781951631291 (trade paperback) | ISBN 9781951631307 (ebook)
Subjects: LCGFT: Poetry.
Classification: LCC PS3616.R5463 R63 2023 (print) | LCC PS3616.R5463 (ebook) | DDC 811/.6—dc23/eng/20220531
LC record available at https://lccn.loc.gov/2022023971
LC ebook record available at https://lccn.loc.gov/2022023972

Published by SFWP
369 Montezuma Ave. #350
Santa Fe, NM 87501
(505) 428-9045
sfwp.com

PRAISE FOR *ROADMAP*

"Monica Prince's *Roadmap* is indeed an extraordinary blueprint of the holy and perilous terrain of Black life and Black love. This slim volume of choreographed poetry feels epic in its power to unearth deep complexities at the intersections of shame and trauma, fear and freedom, hashtags and hallelujahs. In these pages, I am reminded of the god Ntozake Shange told me I would find in myself. And by the end, I couldn't do anything but shout. *Roadmap* is a revelation."

—Deesha Philyaw, author of *The Secret Lives of Church Ladies*

"Monica Prince provides a haunting route through hurt and hope. *Roadmap* guides the reader through the Black experience, linking us through the past and present with character and imagery. Prince gives us a view of what is and the possibility of what is to be. This book looks real good on your bookshelf. Get it wherever you can."

—Omar Holmon, Co-author of *Black Nerd Problems* and author of *We Were All Someone Else Yesterday*

"In *Roadmap*, Monica Prince channels the spirits that undergird our cultural conversations about race, relationships, and inheritance, taking the reader on a profound exploration that balances narrative and atmosphere with deftness. It may be the most impressive work yet in Prince's stellar catalogue of choreopoems."

—Alex Wells Shapiro, author of *Insect Architecture*

"Monica Prince's *Roadmap* is alive on the page, with its beats, silences, and chorus of voices that make me feel I'm in the audience experiencing the staged version of this beautifully-written choreopoem. In this book, Prince "drown[s] in the sticky parts, the urgency of the moment," through surprising music and language that's "slick [like] kisses against...wrists."

As a reader, I am tar-tethered to the moment Raven, the mother of our main character Dorian, laments: "I fell in love with a Black man/and I don't think I'll sleep soundly ever again." Throughout *Roadmap*, Prince encourages us to remember how tightly woven our world is with the one of this choreopoem, as facts and figures about mental health, violence, and maternal mortality pepper a project where "grief is our inheritance" but intergenerational love might be our roadmap to survival."

—Chet'la Sebree, author of *Mistress* and *Field Study,* winner of the 2020 James Laughlin Award from the Academy of American Poets

"In this breathtaking choreopoem, Prince invites us to participate in a sacred necromancy. She exposes the skeletons in our closets, then reminds us yes, dry bones can live. *Roadmap* is at times sorrowful and others joyful, infuriating and a balm – always pushing forward with love and expectation."

—Ashley Lumpkin, author of *I Hate You All Equally*

"*Roadmap* tells the story of a perilous journey between the weight of legacy and the determination toward the future. Throughout the choreopoem, Dorian negotiates the seemingly inevitable inheritance of violence and statistics that continue to stalk him, while the urgency of love and hope urges its light through the cracks with its own kind of force. As he carves a roadmap into his skin to remember all he carries, he creates another in becoming a partner and a father, choosing to find, or even create, a different landscape for himself and his family. As author Monica Prince reminds us in *Roadmap*, "There are Black people in the future.""

—Suzi Q. Smith, author of *A Gospel of Bones* and *Poems for the End of the World*

"*Roadmap* is a lyrical tapestry of the danger lingering behind being Black in the United States. Following an ancestral excavation of that which made him, Dorian is riddled by a number of potholes, daring him to trip and be folded a statistic reckoning with his own Black life. Prince's work does a beautiful job of unfolding pathways for Dorian and his loved ones with the hope of being good, of defying the odds. *Roadmap* will leave you wanting more for yourself, and reminded that we all simply want to grow old and love those around us for all that we are."

—Casey Rocheteau, author of *Gorgoneion* and *The Dozen*

"How does a Black child become themselves? In *Roadmap*, Monica Prince deftly navigates this seemingly straightforward question through all the difficulties seen and unseen, past and present, urgent and necessary. Prince weaves together commanding choreography and remarkable poetry to track the life of Dorian, a young Black man in America; his journey through love, loss, pain, and perseverance grips you from the opening and doesn't let go."

—Cameron Barnett, author of *The Drowning Boy's Guide to Water*

"Monica Prince is a writer that does it all: educates, inspires, and entertains. In her latest work, *Roadmap*, she uses the supernatural to highlight the wholly unnatural specter of premature death that haunts Black men in America with heartbreaking clarity."

—James Stewart III, Writer and Co-Curator of Exhibit B

"Both grueling and reassuring, *Roadmap* explores what it means to be Black in the United States. It urges us to question what we're willing to sacrifice for joy and survival. When tragedy and beauty coexist, how may we spell "hope" in different ways? Challenging stereotypes with facts, Prince invites us to ponder these questions."

—Paloma Sierra, Poet-playwright

"Prince's vision in *Roadmap* shakes us awake, breaks our racing, aching hearts, and recalibrates the brain itself. At the center of this choreopoem are explorations of intergenerational and ancestral trauma and love, queerness, Blackness, and the tragedies, grief, and joys of modern American life that we need now, always, and forever."

—Dr. Katie Jean Shinkle, author of *Thick City* and *Our Prayers After the Fire*

Roadmap is a clear shot ringing into the dark of Black survival. Weaving voices of ancestors and loved ones, Prince stages the likelihood that a young Black man will persevere beyond middle-age. A necessary read and theatrical tool, *Roadmap* targets racism in America."

—Kimberly Ann Priest, author of *Slaughter the One Bird*

"In *Roadmap*, choreopoet Monica Prince lays bare the sins of our nation. What joy, what life, is possible when racism is this deviled sun watching over us from birth to death? What hope is there to have? At times haunting and unsettling, *Roadmap* is fueled by a roaring anger and hard love. Prince dares us to confront our past and present, because without doing so there is no promised future."

—Christopher Gonzalez, author of *I'm Not Hungry But I Could Eat*

AUTHOR'S NOTE

The choreopoem structure and term comes from Ntozake Shange's award-winning choreopoem, *For colored girls who have considered suicide / when the rainbow is enuf* (1975). Rest in power, Sister Shange.

For more information about staging this work, see the end of this book, and please contact admin@sfwp.com for production rights.

POEMS BY TITLE

The Novelist 1

A Child, a Shot, a Name 2

Cloudless Afternoon 5

Roadmap: Family Tree 7

Sex Work Is Real Work 8

Cut 12

Tongues and Tattoos 15

Expectations 17

Call It Love 23

Insomnia, Love, and a Black Man 28

Different 30

Unfinished List of Other Ways
Black Parents Say "I Love You" 41

The Greatest Good 46

Proposal 47

Black Boys are Missing 49

Fight 51

Knives 53

Dance Break 54

The Smallest Map 55

Nursery Rhyme: For Eric Garner 57

On the Outside 60

Do Not Pray 64

Past, Present, Prophecy 66

DRAMATIS PERSONAE

THE NOVELIST – ageless ancestor depicted by a woman of color whose face and skin color are never seen. She wears all black with a hood, gloves, and veil. Fog or light changes mark her entrances and exits, emphasizing her ethereal presence. (Can be played by a nonbinary performer but uses she/her pronouns.)

DORIAN – twenty-something, polyamorous, pansexual Black man. He wears casual clothing (jeans, red t-shirt, sneakers).

BELLE – thirty or forty-something woman of color, DORIAN's grandmother. She wears leggings and an oversized sweater with a lacy bra beneath, no shoes.

NEIL – forty- or fifty-something Black man, DORIAN's father, BELLE's son. He wears semi-casual clothing (pressed jeans, button down shirt, clean sneakers or loafers) and has tattoos all over his body.

RAVEN – forty- or fifty-something Black woman, DORIAN's mother, NEIL's wife. She wears casual clothing (jeans or leggings, bright shirt/blouse or tank top, sandals) and wears her hair naturally.

AISA (pronounced Eye-Shuh) – twenty-something, polyamorous, pansexual woman of color, DORIAN's beloved. She wears casual clothing (leggings, dress with pockets, sandals).

TY – twenty-something, polyamorous, pansexual person of color. They wear black leggings and a black t-shirt, and are barefoot, except when they perform "Do Not Pray." (Can also play DANCER.)

NOELLE – twenty-something, polyamorous, pansexual person of color. They are barefoot and wear black leggings and a black t-shirt. (Can also play DANCER.)

LUTHER – twenty-something, polyamorous, pansexual person of color. They wear black leggings and a black t-shirt, and are barefoot, except when they perform "On the Outside." (Can also play DANCER.)

DANCER(S) – any age, any race (ideally all people of color). They are barefoot and wear black leggings and black t-shirts. (Minimum: 8.)

For Rob—may we survive each other.

"Honey, I said, my life is a ghost story. Then tell it to me, she said."
—Aminata Diallo from *The Book of Negroes* by Lawrence Hill

Lights out. Room fills with fog.
Back doors open. The Novelist enters,
wearing a floor-length black cloak/robe,
black gloves, black shoes, and black
hood. A veil or black paint masks her
face. No part of her skin is visible.
Her very presence unsettles the
audience. She walks down the aisle as
she recites. Her voice is dark and
deep like the unburied of the Middle
Passage. When she reaches the stage,
lights come up; she turns to face the
audience, but her head remains bowed,
and her hands stay either crossed in
front of her chest or in a prayer position.

THE NOVELIST

You do not need to believe in a god
to see me. I exist between blinks,
during the early hours of dawn,
right before sleep leaves your lungs.
I speak in whispers, live on the edges
of your skin, walk through walls.
This is not hyperbole or a metaphor.
If it is easier, call me ancestor, muse,
but god may be too much for your grasp.
If you would rather be precise, call me
ethereal, haunt, immortal challenge
of depth and universe. I am your womb,
your missing rib, your first breath, your fear,
the prayer for safety every time you leave home.
I am conception during *Purple Rain*,
legs split and sliding down a steel pole,
the crown rightfully placed on your head.

I am not a dream. You are not hallucinating.
This is not Hell or Heaven or Purgatory or Nirvana.
No, colored child, I am not an angel or demon,
not a courier between dimensions. I am the novel
of the world, endless passages of every life
before and after you. I know how this ends.
How dirty your hands will be, what good
they will do for us all.

> *The Novelist ascends onto the*
> *stage and stands in the center. The*
> *fog ceases. Dorian enters stage left.*

THE NOVELIST
Here is the ending—

> *Dorian walks around the space.*
> *The Novelist doesn't acknowledge him*
> *as she moves to stand stage left.*

THE NOVELIST
A child.

> *Dorian looks curiously at her.*
> *Then a gunshot is heard.*
> *Dorian falls to the ground.*

THE NOVELIST
A shot.

> *Offstage, a woman's voice shrieks,*
> *"Dorian!" A femme dancer runs on stage*
> *to his aid. She's quickly followed by three*

*more femme dancers who shout different
names: "Trayvon!" "Antwon!" "Tamir!"*

THE NOVELIST
A name.

*The dancers crowd around the body,
hysterical for two beats.*

THE NOVELIST
I say name.

*The dancers stop and stand in a rectangle
around Dorian, facing the audience. He
stands and moves to the short edge of the
rectangle downstage, facing the audience.*

THE NOVELIST
But I mean: hash tag.

*As dancers shout the following
lines, Dorian trust falls into
the femme dancers' arms.
They carry him offstage left.*

DANCERS (*offstage or from back of the room, with increasing fervor*)
#BlackLivesMatter
#SayHerName
#RestInPower
#BlackLivesMatter
#SayHerName
#RestInPower
#BlackLivesMatter

#SayHerName
#RestInPower

THE NOVELIST *(once silent)*
His name is Dorian,
and you know where it starts—
a Native scalped, an African snatched,

wars and blood and bodies lined from sea
to shining sea. You only listen to the song of the missing.
I have learned to sing in the voices of the dead,

to rifle through graves and brush off headstones
until I find the ones that belong to me.
They all belong to me—the fallen, the slain,

the broken and tired and joyful and excellent.
He is excellent, Dorian. And you know how he dies.
It is good. It is a good death. The same one

we all accept with our bodies stained by melanin,
the same map made of history stitched in our cells.
There are Black people in the future.

They grow up. They grow old. You have a choice—
will you love him now, when he can still smell
the flowers you present, or will you only love him

later, a hashtag for the cause, another morsel
stuck in the bloody teeth of white supremacy's maw?
Remember his name—Dorian. Remember his breath,

his laughter, his luxury made flesh. He exists
in the future. And his death is good.
It is good. Believe me, when he dies,

it is good.

The Novelist moves to the audience.
Dancers enter from offstage and the back
of the room and dance as Dorian's body
is returned to stage by the dancers from
stage left. They lower him back to the
floor at centerstage. Some dancers get
on stage, and they all dance around his
body. Suddenly, rapid gunfire is heard,
and everyone collapses. The Novelist
stands in the audience stage left. Beat.

THE NOVELIST
Okay, colored child—be good.

All dancers and Dorian rise.

THE NOVELIST
Be good.

DANCER 1
There is always something to say

DANCER 2
when a fire breaks out.

DANCER 3
When sirens wail

DANCER 4
and lights blind

DANCER 5
and water smothers the flames—

DANCER 6
there is always something to say.

DANCER 7
Empty apologies,

DANCER 8
bitter tongues.

DANCER 9
The world is on fire,

DANCER 10
but all anyone can say is,

ALL DANCERS *(pointing up to the sky, wistfully)*
Look how cloudless the sky.

*Dancers exit by wandering around
pointing to the sky, asking the audience
if they can see any clouds, acting
awestruck by the lack of them. Some
sit in the audience while others exit
completely. Dorian remains center stage
and looks directly at The Novelist.*

THE NOVELIST
Where did you come from, colored child?
What bones broke to make you?
Let us begin.

> *The Novelist exits out the back of*
> *the room. Dorian watches her leave.*

DORIAN
The blueprint for the house where love lives
is stamped on my DNA. My skeleton is the rebar
in the walls, my blood the mortar between bricks.
I learned love from the bodies who fashioned me,
whose choices funneled through generations.
They are my roadmap. A family tree
strewn across street signs and construction zones,
etched on the insides of my hands. I follow
the tire tracks back to the first acceleration.
Whose bones broke to make mine?
Watch.

> *Belle, Neil, Raven, and Aisa enter*
> *from stage right. They stand in a*
> *line facing the audience. As Dorian*
> *introduces them, he walks behind them.*

DORIAN
My grandmother, Belle.

BELLE
I can only trace our family history
to an island behind God's back.
But blood makes it hard to see
past Great-Granny and whoever raped her.

DORIAN
My parents, Raven and Neil.

RAVEN
You couldn't wait to recite me poetry
about placenta and fetal backflips.

NEIL
A good man, my son. A good man.

DORIAN
My beloved, Aisa.

AISA
My body registered yours and started humming.
I could sing along, it was so loud.

DORIAN
Nature versus nurture.
Is melanin my death sentence?

> *All exit stage right except Belle.*
> *Dancer enters stage left with a chair and*
> *exits stage right. Belle recites and dances*
> *using the chair, Janet Jackson-style.*

BELLE
They call me all kinds of things,
but you can call me Belle.
Named not for the fairy tale, but the simplicity:
beautiful in French. Every child is named

Hope, but we each spell it differently.

I'll never meet my grandson. I don't know how
they will say his name.

I respond to whatever they pay me
to be called. I'm supposed to like it.
No one really cares if I don't—they care
if I can't pretend. Then, the violence starts:
a hand across the face, teeth puncturing the skin,
the snarl of *nigger bitch* in the air. People still think
money lets you own someone,
like a few crumpled bills crushed into my palm
bequeaths you the title of *Master.*

DANCERS *(offstage or in audience, chanting)*
Sex work is real work.

BELLE
I am no one's slave.

DANCERS *(offstage or in audience, chanting)*
Sex work is real work.

BELLE
I am no one's property.

DANCERS *(offstage or in audience, chanting)*
Sex work is real work.

BELLE
I am damn good at what I do.

I never told Neil who his father was.
But he knows the man was a client. Knows
someone paid to use me so I could send him
to school with clean clothes and a full stomach.
Truth be told—I don't know which client
he looks like. Their faces all turn to sand
after the money is spent. I want you to know:
I'm not a sex worker who didn't have a choice.
I don't do this because I hate myself. Rather,
my legs spread and my back arches and my voice sings
because it feels *good*. And with this skin so Black,
this body so woman—shouldn't *something* feel good?

Dancer enters stage right. Belle freezes.

DANCER
Compared to other women in other professions, prostitution is the one in
which women are most likely to be murdered. However, the vast majority
of women who enter prostitution leave the trade alive.

*Dancer exits stage right. Belle unfreezes
and sits in the chair backwards.
Neil enters stage right and crosses the
stage, watching Belle on the chair.*

BELLE
Five years sober—that's what we say
when we stop working, no clients or ads or solicitations.
For my colored child, now a man, now chasing
his own feel-good. I like to believe I did right
most of his life, provided, loved hard.
All so he can survive me.
I refuse to scream his name in the street,
my hands drenched in his blood,

his eyes flickering out.
I deserve that, as his mother.
He deserves that, as my son,
to bury me, not vice versa.

Neil exits stage left.

*Belle stands and crosses the stage.
She then runs and jumps onto the
chair, tipping it over. As it clatters
beneath her, a shotgun blast is heard,
and she falls to her knees. She leans back
onto the floor and breathes slowly.*

BELLE
It's always a gun.
Americans love their guns.
Love to see what holes they make
in the bodies of the expendable.
But you can't throw me away.
I'm a Black woman.
I already broke the world.

*Belle stops breathing. Dancers enter
from stage right, lift her body, and carry
her and the chair offstage right. Fog
rolls in and The Novelist enters at
the back of the room, then begins
walking down the aisle as she recites.*

THE NOVELIST
Show us the stereotype:
Sex worker knocked up by a client.
Shot to death in her own home.

So far, so expected, this map too predictable.
I said be good, colored child.
Show me good.

> *The Novelist ascends the stage and exits*
> *as fog stops. Neil enters stage left and*
> *a dancer enters stage right. Neil has a*
> *razor blade in his hands that he fiddles*
> *with but never uses. Occasionally, he*
> *shows off his tattoos on his arms.*

DANCER
Many children of sex workers experience extreme vulnerabilities, such as
low school enrollment, psychosocial issues, and social marginalization.
Drug use, sexual abuse, violent tendencies, and social alienation are also
likely developments in these children.

> *Dancer exits stage right.*

NEIL
At eleven, I cut myself on a razor someone left in the bathroom sink.
My mother was asleep. It wasn't her razor. It felt good—
at first. Then slithered in shame. I'm not supposed
to like this. But cutting helped me disappear
into the whiteness preferred of me.

But not by my mother—who, most days,
loved this country. She never taught me
to hate the police or burn flags,
but when it came to existing while Black,
she asked me to hold still, never raise my voice.

In college, my Black professor warned me of a KKK sect
rooted at the edge of town. There, I added

rope to my list of bodily fears, after *water, white hoods,*
and *trees.* I do not trust any person that wears hate
like a badge of honor, masking fear of the other as pride.

Ever since blade released blood from my skin,
I haven't been able to relax my spine in public.
What if someone discovers the trenches I've carved
in my arms, stomach, and hips? Who will tell my mother
her son is a map of every way Black men can die?

Before she passed, my mother was sober. No more clients,
no more strangers leaving razors in the bathroom.
Not that it mattered. By then, highways illuminated my skin,
leading to self-preservation, constantly under construction.
Like her, I worry if naming my child signs their death warrant.

Maybe that's just the risk of having a Black child. I'm not immune
to all the ways the world disrupts my peace, how it burrows
into my cells. But I've since traded razors for needles
filled with ink, drawn pictures on this body to immortalize
the perforations I scratched for whoever comes to tear me apart.

It should be harder to find them now, to separate
my flesh from my blood. Let it be known: innocence
is not the line in the sand for the end of childhood.
As if the worst way to grow up is to be ripped from it,
typically by someone who had theirs ruined, too.

But if we are all refugees of our childhoods,
drifting forever outside of that place, balanced
on the line of innocence and whatever comes next,
I'm not surprised by the moon, dictating
blood and ocean. I'm not even surprised by

what had to be my mother's undoing—a man,
a gun, her skin too dark and her sex
too loud. She tried. I know that's nearly all

I could expect from her, to do and have done her best,
to never identify my remains should I die first.

She got her wish—to never have to mourn her baby
or learn the name of the coward who took him from her.
But now I live without her, my body scarred over
with new melanin, tattoos like liquid bandages keeping me intact,
her memory a promise to never abandon my own kid.

I want to be enough for the child I bring into this suffering,
be able to vow not to smoke
or leave without saying goodbye. I can only hope
I can do it—bring someone here,
trust I won't do more damage.

Dancer enters stage right.

DANCER
Although Black youth have historically not been considered at high risk for
suicide and self-harm, current trends now challenge that. The Congressional
Black Caucus and the Youth Risk Behavior Survey, developed by the CDC,
both reported that Black males are engaging in more lethal means when
attempting suicide. Self-harm is considered a "white thing," and the stigma
around mental health in the Black community prevents many Black youth
from reporting their challenges with self-harm and suicidal ideation.

*Dancer approaches Neil and takes the
razor from him, who hands it over at first
reluctantly, then resolutely. He nods at
the dancer that then exits stage right. Neil
remains on stage while Raven enters from
the back of the room. While they recite,
Raven makes her way to the stage.*

RAVEN

Our lives are divided into two parts:
before Dorian, and after.

NEIL

Before Dorian, you were my feel-good.
To call you an escape would cheapen the joy.
Life was always a little enflamed, a series of open wounds
charred at the edges. I learned to stay inside the blood,
where it's warm, where immunity multiplies.

RAVEN

Before Dorian, I wanted stories. You told me once
that love has no rules, just pulsing need.
It's possible to break a heart by accident, to walk away
in the middle out of fear. But you didn't do that.
For five years before Dorian, you didn't leave.

Raven gets on stage
and dances with Neil.

NEIL

You're drunk, and it's midnight.
You want stories, so you peel my shirt off,
begging me to show you what ink does to skin,
did to this body. You don't ask why
there are so many tattoos, or what they hide.
I couldn't tell you if you did. Not yet.
To this day, you still ignore my past pain,
believe me stronger than yesterday would suggest.

RAVEN

I'm drunk, and it's midnight.
You want to feel good, so you let me undress you,
slide my painted nails against every image and outline,
my body melting into yours. I cannot tell you
why my orgasms sound like grenades shattering
century-old foundation, don't want you
to imagine me unstable, ruined. I whisper the word
survivor into your collarbone—a promise, a kinship.

NEIL

You lick each syllable, trace each picture
with your pointed tongue, pull the scars right out of me.
We drown in the sticky parts, the urgency of the moment,
what was supposed to be another harmless night turning permanent.

RAVEN

In the morning, I already know we're in the after.

NEIL

My skin wears your name,
and I can't scrub you off.

> *Neil and Raven stand together in the*
> *center. Neil rubs his hand over Raven's*
> *belly, and they smile at each other.*

RAVEN

I'll name him Dorian.

NEIL

A gift—from the sea.

RAVEN
Just like his daddy.

NEIL
Just like his legacy.

> *Dorian enters at the back of*
> *the room and stays there.*

DORIAN
When it comes to Black families,
the version you expect looks like this:

> *Neil and Raven's body language changes.*
> *Neil looks enraged and she looks scared.*
> *They move away from each other, and*
> *Neil pulls out a flask and starts to drink.*
> *Raven becomes visibly anxious.*

DORIAN
Father's a drunk.
Mother's a coward.

NEIL *(shouting at Raven)*
You don't understand!
Everyone's against the Black man—the white man,
the white woman, you!

RAVEN
Don't you mean the Black woman,
who's always right here?
Standing with you?

NEIL
Standing *on* me!

Neil puts the flask back in his pocket and reaches for Raven. They begin an abusive dance in the style of the violent French apache, as Neil tries to hit her but continues to miss while Raven evades his blows and tries to calm him.

RAVEN *(dismissive)*
You're drunk.

NEIL
You're a cheating bitch!

RAVEN *(incredulous)*
What?!

NEIL
That baby's not mine! I know it's not!

RAVEN *(desperate)*
What? Whose else could it be?

NEIL
Shut up!

RAVEN
I crave you like air.

Look what I give up,
how I sacrifice myself for you to absorb me,
what little is left of me every morning.

NEIL
I said, shut up!

RAVEN
Who else could I want but you,
who else could bloom a baby inside me,
shattered and beautiful as you are?

NEIL
Shut the fuck up!

RAVEN *(snarling, sarcastic)*
Oh—so, that's how it's gonna be, huh?
I'm supposed to take your bullshit,
love you anyway, believe you always?
Follow your GPS into Hell?
A woman should praise the man—the king, right?

NEIL
King ... yes!
I know that baby isn't mine—
these hos ain't loyal.

RAVEN
Ride or die, right, baby?

NEIL
Damn straight!

Neil finally succeeds in hitting Raven.
She tumbles to the ground. She
immediately clutches her abdomen,
worried for the baby. Neil stands
over her, breathing heavily,
clenching and unclenching his fists.
She looks up at him with rage.

DORIAN
Or, you expect this version:
Father is abusive.
Mother is defensive.

RAVEN *(angrily, to herself)*
The first time is the last time.

NEIL *(still pissed)*
What?

RAVEN *(standing slowly, hand still on her belly, not looking at Neil, angry)*
The first time is the last time.

NEIL *(suddenly a little worried, stepping back)*
C'mon, Raven, chill. It was an accident.

Raven walks toward Neil as he steps back
from her, his hands up. She pulls a knife
from her bra and unsnaps it. Neil looks
at the knife and back at her several times.

RAVEN

I told you—if you *ever* put hands on me,
you would not survive to apologize.

NEIL

Baby, I'm sorry. Now, put that down.
You know how I feel about knives.

RAVEN

Yes, I do. Who do you think you're fucking with?

NEIL

Hey...calm down. Let's talk about this.

RAVEN

Now you wanna talk?
When you're scared of me?
I'm on the ground, face stinging,
and you ain't got shit to say.
I'm holding the knife—and suddenly,
you got words?

NEIL

Raven, I'm sorry.

RAVEN *(measured)*

Get out.

*Neil stands still, looking between her
and the knife. Raven lunges at him
with the knife, and he jumps back.*

RAVEN *(screaming)*
Get the fuck out!

> *Neil drops his hands and takes a breath as Raven stares at him, her hand visibly shaking with the knife. He starts to say something, then sighs. He exits stage right. Raven watches him leave. She trembles violently as she drops the knife and collapses to the floor, sobbing.*

DORIAN
Or, you expect this:
Father is absent.
Mother's a statistic.

> *After several beats, Raven calms and stands. She rubs her belly. A dancer enters stage right. After a beat, Raven and the dancer spin together a few times, then the dancer hands Raven a swaddled child and exits stage right, taking the knife.*

DORIAN
But that's not what happened.

> *Neil returns from stage right and stands with Raven, holding the baby. They smile, kiss, and fawn over the child briefly, then exit stage right, Neil slapping Raven's butt playfully on their way out.*

DORIAN *(moving onto the stage)*
My instinct is to defend her first.
To assume he beat her or cheated or left.
Everyone said that's what happens
to Black families: alcohol, abuse, abandonment.

DANCER *(offstage or in audience)*
"Black love is black wealth." –Nikki Giovanni

DORIAN
In my house, we bathed in love.
But grief is our inheritance, cluttering
every corner, showing up like anger
in my blood, like distraction at school.
In a meeting with my guidance counselor and teachers,
they once asked,

DANCERS *(in audience or offstage, high-pitched, seemingly innocuous)*
What's it like at home?

> *Raven and Neil enter with dancers from*
> *audience and stage right. They dance*
> *around and with Dorian as he recites.*

DORIAN
Most nights, my parents would sing together,
the walls shaking with what they called love. In the kitchen,
she'd dab whipped cream on his nose,
or he'd smack her ass on his way past.
They were always smiling through these little flirts,
these small love taps. It's supposed to be love.

As a child on the playground, flirting is punching someone
and running away. Biting their fingers during lunch.
Yanking them off the swing mid-flight and laughing
when tears parade down their face.
Abuse is love, we all learned.
This is how I drew the blueprint for the house
where love lives, another kind of map.
In my house, hugs followed slaps,
curses came before winks, blood painted every kiss.

> *Dancers pair up and synchronize*
> *mimed violent dance on stage and*
> *in audience. One dancer is submissive*
> *while the other is dominant. Neil*
> *is submissive and Raven is dominant.*
> *Dorian stands centerstage.*

DANCER *(offstage or in audience)*
1 in 15 children are exposed to intimate partner violence each year, and
90% are witnesses to the violence.

DORIAN
If they aren't crying, they don't love you.

DANCER *(offstage or in audience)*
Abused children are more likely to exhibit violent behavior.

DORIAN
If their skin doesn't open, they don't love you.

DANCER *(offstage or in audience)*
Children raised in abusive homes equate violence with problem-solving.

DORIAN
If there isn't blood, they don't love you.

Their throat has to curdle around a scream,
one so piercing, it soundtracks your nightmares.

If they won't scream,
they don't love you.

So, make them—

Submissive dancing partners all shriek.

DORIAN
—love you.

*Dancers end with submissive partner
on the ground and dominant partner
standing over them with a hand at
their throat, both struggling. All hold
for a beat. Dorian looks around,
horrified. Fog rolls onto the stage and
The Novelist enters stage right.*

THE NOVELIST
Toxic, yes?

DORIAN
I grew out of this childish shit.

THE NOVELIST
If it is childish, why are they all dead?

*Dominant dancers and Raven
release the submissive ones and
exit. Submissive dancers lie gravely
still. Dorian looks panicked.*

DANCER *(offstage or in audience)*
1 in 3 female murder victims are killed by their partners. 1 in 20 male
murder victims are killed by their partners.

DORIAN
But my parents won't kill each other.
A little bickering, some rough teasing—that's not a murder plot.
Like, that's just how they love.

*Submissive dancers and Neil all
stand and slowly close in on Dorian.*

DANCER 1
That's just how they love.

DANCER 2
It's not serious.

DANCER 3
They don't actually *hit* me.

NEIL
It never hurts.

DANCER 4
That's just how they love.

DANCER 1
It's all in good fun.

DANCER 2
We're just playing around.

DANCER 3
Doesn't even leave a mark.

NEIL
I've seen worse.

DANCER 4
That's just how they love.

ALL DANCERS and NEIL
That's just how they love.
That's just how they love.
That's just how they love.

*Dancers and Neil close in on Dorian as
they repeat the line until he shouts and
collapses. They stand around him for a
beat. As The Novelist crosses to Dorian,
the dancers make space for her. She
stands near Dorian until he realizes no
one is hurting him. He stops cowering*

*and looks around. He notices The
Novelist and quickly scrambles to his feet.*

THE NOVELIST
Grow out of this, colored child.
Abuse is a cycle rarely broken cleanly.

DORIAN
I'll need to retrain my hands.

THE NOVELIST
Train them for good.

*The Novelist exits with Neil and
dancers out the back of the room. As
they leave, Dorian crosses to the edge of
the stage and sits down, clenching and
unclenching his hands. Raven enters but
doesn't notice Dorian. When she speaks,
Dorian looks up and watches her as
if he's intruding on a rare moment.*

RAVEN
In the dark, my beloved sleeps easily. I can't imagine how.
Prone to tears in public and clutching him desperately,
I lie awake, counting my heartbeats in time
to his inhale ... exhale ... inhale. As a child, white spaces
enveloped me. I convinced myself that my dark body
would fare safer in the presence of the oppressors.
I was wrong.

The first white boy I ever loved carried a knife to school
every day. Called it protection. Should have called it a promise
to bring a gun tomorrow. And then, he did.

He killed a boy his age over some weed—
two in the chest, one in the head. Sounded like a rap song,
a bad cop drama. I couldn't love him anymore after
I saw what his hands were capable of, what they had always
been able to do. What privilege, an inheritance
he never questioned. Generations of bad behavior, entitlement,
and misplaced rage taught him to solve fear with violence,
to take what's his even if it doesn't belong to him.

The last white man I ever loved
did exactly what I expected him to do,
what every story that starts with murder must include.
He knew he could do whatever he wanted
because every man before him had done the same thing.
Of course his body could rape and pillage.
What else was it made for?

Beat.

This is not to say that white men cannot be loved.
That colored girls like me cannot open for them, produce
legacies of joy with them, plot new maps of uncharted territory,
where they can escape the damage they wreak.
No, I mean, I cannot celebrate another Loving Day
as someone's rebellious streak, risk a racist grandparent
bleaching my baby's skin in the bathtub, defend a ballot cast
in favor of my extermination. I mean—
I fell in love with a Black man,
and I don't think I'll sleep soundly ever again.

*Neil enters stage right and dances
with Raven for remainder of poem.*

RAVEN

I worry for my beloved Black man, asleep beside me,
father of my child, someone's son and brother and friend.
I want to keep loving him, to accept the probability
that the anger of a bitter white man might force him
out of my bed and into the ground too soon.
Love isn't logical here, as it conquers the possibility
of irrevocable loss. I can't help myself.
He's just so miraculous.

> *Fog rolls in and The Novelist enters
> at the back of the room. Dorian
> stands and tries to catch Raven and Neil,
> but they are lost in each other and
> exit stage right too quickly. He begins
> to say something to his parents but stops
> when he hears The Novelist's voice.*

THE NOVELIST

Loving any person means coming to terms with the likelihood
that they may have assaulted someone before they met you.
When it comes to love, there are no clean hands.

> *The Novelist exits and the fog
> stops. Dorian stares down at his
> hands. Aisa, Noelle, Luther, and
> Ty enter stage right. Dorian moves
> among them throughout the poem.*

DORIAN

Love takes practice.
New maps drawn for fresh lovers.
Each lesson harder than the last, each partner

full of panic and desire and a need to be touched,
considered, focused on for just a few minutes.

AISA
Attention is the most basic form of love—

DORIAN
and I love all of you: shy, confident, pretty,
awkward, abused, violent, scared. Mostly—mostly scared.

NOELLE
We taste like progress.

DORIAN
Each partner more desperate
to take care of me, to keep me safe.

LUTHER
Isn't that always our job?

TY
To make sure *you* survive, *you* recover,
you come first?

DORIAN
Yes.

All stop dancing, turn to look
at Dorian, irritated.

DORIAN
I want to say I'm different, nothing like
what Drake tells you to expect from me.

AISA *(with attitude)*
Liar.

NOELLE *(convinced)*
Cheater.

LUTHER *(caustic)*
Fuckboi.

TY *(as expected)*
Ain't shit.

DORIAN
So tonight, I'm different.

> *Dorian and Aisa resume dancing.*
> *Noelle, Luther, and Ty drift*
> *upstage, standing in a line evenly*
> *spaced, hands crossed in front of*
> *their chests, looking on neutrally.*

DORIAN
Right now, the moon lights up the whole room
and wraps you in gold, baby girl. I could tell you
how beautiful you are, that making your body
hum to the beat of pulse and lung is my only priority,
that I've never tasted pink quite like yours.

And I will. I will drench you in compliments
until the bed becomes an ocean and your gasps
my life jacket. If that's what you want,
to feel singular and worshipped, told jewels
gleam between your thighs, that I'm tasked
with shining them until they blind any wandering glance—
I will do that tonight. For you.
Give me your enthusiastic yes, and I will worship you.

> *Dorian and Aisa stop dancing.*
> *Dorian drifts away from her and*
> *upstage toward Noelle, Luther, and*
> *Ty, who independently engage*
> *with him as he moves between them.*

DORIAN
It's tomorrow you should worry about,
the morning like a slap, hot and real. When I whisper
out of bed, into clothes, out the front door.
When I repeat every dirty detail on another body,
in another apartment, in another city. When you ask
why and I say *why not.*

> *Dorian moves back downstage*
> *but not close to Aisa.*

AISA *(convinced)*
Liar.

NOELLE *(annoyed)*
Cheater.

LUTHER *(with attitude)*
Fuckboi.

TY *(told you so)*
Ain't shit.

DORIAN *(to Aisa)*
I'm not trying to hurt you.

> *Noelle, Luther, and Ty walk*
> *toward Aisa.*

DANCER *(offstage or in audience)*
Individuals who cheat are 3.5 times more likely to cheat in a subsequent relationship.

DORIAN *(aside)*
Depends what you call cheating.

AISA *(to audience)*
Depends what you call relationship.

> *Dorian looks at Aisa, surprised.*

DORIAN
It's just how I'm built. I can't help myself.

AISA *(incredulous)*
You can't help yourself?

Dorian reaches for Ty, Noelle,
and Luther, and dances them
across the stage.

DORIAN
I love their hips, their hands,
the St. Louis Arch of their spines.
I can't help but touch them,
slick kisses against their wrists, collarbones,
nipples, lips, heads. I'm addicted
to their moans, every shuddered gasp,
their ecstasy another high from night to night.
I just can't help it.

DANCER *(in audience)*
Ay girl, yo' mama let you date?

DORIAN
Not like that.

DANCER *(in audience)*
Hey papi, why don't you walk past again?

DORIAN
C'mon, not like that.

DANCER *(in audience)*
Whatcho man got to do wit me?

DORIAN
Seriously, I'm different.
I'm not like that.

AISA
But you just said—

ALL *except Dorian*
I can't help myself.

> *Dorian drops the hand of the person*
> *he's dancing with and stands tall.*

AISA *(resolute)*
Liar.

NOELLE *(resolute)*
Cheater.

LUTHER *(resolute)*
Fuckboi.

TY *(resolute)*
Ain't shit.

> *Luther and Ty saunter off stage right.*
> *Aisa walks downstage and splits center*
> *with Dorian as Noelle walks up behind*
> *her. They all freeze as fog rolls in, and*
> *The Novelist enters at the back of the*

*room. She gravitates toward the stage as
she speaks, and the next few lines unfold.*

THE NOVELIST
You are not so base
that you cannot control your impulses.
Your default is not cheater, is not rapist.
It is easy to repeat rape culture
like there is nothing to be done about it.
Be honest.

All unfreeze.

DORIAN *(to Aisa)*
I don't want to be monogamous.

AISA
Neither do I.

Noelle and Aisa grab hands.

DORIAN
But I don't want you to be with anyone else.

AISA *(scoffs)*
That's called a double standard.

THE NOVELIST
I said, be good, colored child.

DORIAN
But—

AISA
No.

> *Noelle and Aisa share a long passionate
> kiss. Dorian looks on briefly, then
> turns away, conflicted. Fog stops. The
> Novelist comes onto the stage. She
> faces him with hard body language, as
> if to say, "Do not fuck this up." She taps
> Noelle, who breaks the kiss with
> Aisa, and they both exit stage right.
> Aisa advances toward Dorian.*

AISA
You don't get both.

DORIAN
But—

AISA
No.
My time, my love, my body—they're all
just as valuable as yours, magnificent as you may be.
I won't keep saying yes, stay loyal,
remain a wound for your salty tears.
Just because the world beats you
for being Black doesn't mean
you get to control me for being woman.

Aisa grabs Dorian's hand and
places it around her throat.

AISA *(snarling)*
You want to control someone?

Aisa sinks to her knees with Dorian's
hand still wrapped around her throat.

AISA
Fine.
But don't expect love.
Don't expect me to stick around,
to upgrade you while you drain me.
Don't expect surrender to grow
where you've planted resentment.

Aisa tightens Dorian's grip.

AISA *(snarling)*
I am not a game, Dorian.
Don't. Play. Me.

Dorian stands above Aisa for a beat.

DORIAN
I don't want to hurt you.

AISA *(sweeter)*
And what, my love, do you call *hurt*?

> *Dorian looks down at Aisa for a beat, still holding onto her throat. As the next few lines unfold, Dorian dissociates. He appears stressed, angry, and erratic, but he doesn't let go of Aisa's throat, squeezing it tighter and tighter. She remains calm at first, expecting him to mentally return to her.*

DANCER *(offstage or in audience)*
Black women are more likely to be murdered by their male partners than women of any other race.

AISA
Silence never soothes suffering.

DANCER *(offstage or in audience)*
Due to cultural norms of masculinity and victimization, many young men of color do not identify as "victims," even when describing experiences of being harmed.

AISA
I can't help if you don't talk.

DANCER *(offstage or in audience)*
Depression typically manifests as an increase in aggressive and reckless behavior in men, especially in Black men, decreasing its likelihood to be diagnosed.

AISA *(a little worried)*
Are you really going to hurt me?

DANCER *(offstage or in audience)*
Within Black communities, depression is a character flaw. Depressed Black men are labeled as weak, so when they exhibit hyper-aggressive behavior, it's not seen as a symptom of depression. Rather, the behavior is dismissed as normal due to racist stereotypes internalized by the Black community.

AISA *(scared, then shouting)*
Dorian? *(beat)*
Dorian? *(beat)*
Dorian!

> *At the shouting of his name,*
> *Dorian snaps out of the moment and*
> *looks down at Aisa. They both*
> *freeze. Raven and Neil enter from*
> *opposite sides of the back of the room.*

RAVEN
Did you get enough to eat?

NEIL
Pull your pants up, boy.

RAVEN
You can't spend the whole day in bed.

NEIL
Call me if you need a ride home.

RAVEN
You don't want to end up like Cousin Mike—locked up. And for what?

NEIL

In this house, we don't back down from a fight. Hit him back next time!

RAVEN

No one's gonna love you if you keep acting like that.

NEIL

Walk in the corner.

RAVEN

You're gonna have to work twice as hard to get half as much as these white folks.

NEIL

Be safe walking down the street.

RAVEN

Keep your hands out of your pockets.

NEIL

Where's your wallet? Take it off that chain.

RAVEN

You can't wear hoodies anymore.

NEIL

I heard a siren, so I wanted to see where you are.

RAVEN

Repeat our phone number back to me. And Grandma's. You know who to call, right?

NEIL

Who's all gon' be over there? Nah, that Malik boy is trouble. I don't want you at his house. Because I said so!

RAVEN

I'll drive you; I don't want you walking in that neighborhood. You might get lost.

NEIL

Text me when you get home.

RAVEN

Call me when your plane lands.

NEIL

You have enough for groceries this week?

RAVEN

We're praying for you down at the church.

NEIL

The phone works both ways, you know.

RAVEN

Take care of yourself.

NEIL
Get home safe.

RAVEN
Take care of yourself.

NEIL
Get home safe.

RAVEN
Take care of yourself.

NEIL
Get home safe.

RAVEN and NEIL
Don't die.
Don't die.
Don't die.
Don't die.
Don't die.

RAVEN *(voice cracking)*
Please ... just get home in one piece.

> *Dorian and Aisa unfreeze. Dorian looks
> down at Aisa's terrified face and snatches
> his hand away from her. He stumbles
> back a few steps. Aisa coughs and leans
> forward, trying to recover from being
> choked. Raven and Neil exit out the back*

of the room. For a few beats, Dorian
looks between his hands and Aisa.
Finally, he wipes them on his chest and
crosses back to Aisa. He offers his hand to
help her up. She looks carefully at it, then
accepts cautiously and stands up. They
drop hands, not breaking eye contact.

AISA
You say you're different.

DORIAN
I am. I mean, I'm trying to be.

AISA
I want more than different.
I want extraordinary.

DORIAN
And what makes you so special?

AISA
I'm a metaphor, baby.
Beautiful things deserve beautiful things.
And I—I deserve it all.

Dorian and Aisa step toward
one another. Dorian circles
her throughout the poem.

AISA
At first, I couldn't tell whether
the vibration in my blood came from you.
In the mornings, I roll over and my touch
always makes you moan. You're the reason
I can't sleep alone anymore. When we met,
my whole body went up in flames. I thought
everyone in that room would die. You told me,

DORIAN (*as if in her ear*)
I want to build something with you.

AISA
I had no idea you wanted me to be
the stone, mortar, and paint.

At first, I couldn't tell whether
sex was love, if all my plans to protect myself
mattered when I met you. Here's what
I know: my life had no elevation until
you kissed me. My true north, your body engulfs me,
and I let it. I'm prepared to be consumed,
to be overwhelmed until I can't move,
until I have no choice but to become
whatever it is you want me to be.

At first, I couldn't tell whether
surviving a love that splits my atoms
until I am just disjointed matter floating
above the bed we share
was worth it.

DORIAN
And now?

AISA
And now, I know
being worthy is not the point.
It's choice. And I choose you.
I am spectacular—the greatest good.
You are foolish not to worship me.

> *Dorian stands behind Aisa, his arms*
> *circling her waist, holding her tightly.*

DORIAN *(smiling)*
Like a subject worships his queen?

AISA *(serious)*
No.
Like a man worships God.

> *Dorian releases Aisa and takes her hand.*

DORIAN
Terrified and thankful?

AISA *(shakes head no)*
Always getting better.

> *Dorian nods. He gets down on one*
> *knee with Aisa's hand still in his.*

DORIAN
May my love for you meditate across my tongue
like a perpetual prayer. I want every part of you,
perfect and loud. If you open, I will enter,

a willing participant in this sorcery, this explosion,
this body built of blue and bone. May the map
we draw together lead our children home, a compass
tattooed in our smiles, our joy. I cannot scrub you
from my pores, now stained with your magic.
Take me from this Earth
if ever I should try.

AISA *(snarky and smiling)*
Damn straight.

> *Laughing, Dorian stands and*
> *spins Aisa off stage right.*
> *The Novelist enters stage left.*

THE NOVELIST
I see you finding some feel-good for yourself, colored child.
Do not put her on a pedestal,
or call her Queen instead of by her name.
Rather, treat her like she saved your life,
like she will die for you,
as every Black woman has done before her.
But will you do the same, Dorian?
What will you sacrifice for this joy?

> *Dancer enters stage left.*

DANCER
The leading cause of death for Black boys under the age of 13 is suicide.

> *Dorian balks at what he's heard*
> *but before he can clarify, The*
> *Novelist and dancer exit stage right.*

DORIAN

I know a lie or two about Black folk,
about our likelihood to remove one another
from the planet. Not by gang violence
or a jury conviction. A quiet formula
we exchange without language. I know
I'm not the only one with a razor
locked under my bed—

and yet, the statistics have me believing
self-harm is a whites-only phenomenon.
My father carved x's into his skin.
My mother dated white men in hopes they'd kill her.
I don't want to know
these secrets, don't want to inherit
this legacy of scar and reckless, find new ways
to bleed, down tranqs instead of facing reality.
They say we do this for attention—
I do this for strength, for rest,
for freedom. One day, I'll rejoice at my own sobriety:
zero days self-harming, no fantasies

of how to press the eject button from Earth.
You're uncomfortable. Of course—once you know
someone wants to cease to be, you can't unknow.
Can't quell the fact that not everyone wants to hold on
to the end, get from A to Z. You expect bad days, sure,

but not bad enough to end your life, to imagine
waltzing into the sea, stones tied around your waist,
or overdosing on vodka and pills, or jumping from a bridge
into southbound lanes. That feeling of helplessness
you dismiss as a bad day? It boomerangs in my bone marrow,
the double helix of DNA and generational trauma.

Our parents teach fear, not pleasure, death
because of our race an unasked-for burden.

We'll quote a phone number, offer an ear
or shoulder, just enough to soothe
our egos, then move on. Exactly—so useless.
We're aware of echoes of agony, desperate tweets
at zero hour, then we stay shocked at the funeral.

I'm not blaming anyone. I'm not even asking
for help. I want recognition, realization
that young Black boys kill themselves.
That we're more lethal, more successful at it.
One moment, we're in love, laughing, joking—
the next, someone comes across our quieting pulse.

What I'm trying to say is—I'm always angry.
I contain my fury with brutality against my own sparkling.
It hurts. I hurt. I cry. I don't want you to know that.
I know how toxic I sound, but I'm sick of lying
about how much my soul burns. All this
vicarious sorrow—I can't support it.
And occasionally I want to quit, go to glory,
as Grandma might say. But today, today
is a good goddamn day. Today, I thwart any bait
to kill this body. Today, I jazz and swoon,
as I know what I'll do soon.

The Novelist enters stage left
with a dancer.

DANCER
Depression typically manifests as an increase in aggressive and reckless
behavior in men, especially in Black men, decreasing its likelihood to
be diagnosed. In Black communities, therapy and other mental health
services are considered a "white thing," as if depression, anxiety, PTSD, and
other mental illnesses are a luxury afforded only by those not plagued by

institutional racism. Black men underreport their struggles to avoid having their masculinity called into question.

Dancer exits.

THE NOVELIST
Colored child, what good can you conjure
when you cannot love your own body?
How will you save us when you cannot save yourself?

Dorian starts to respond but a gaggle of dancers enters from the back of the room, talking and laughing indistinctly, taking his attention. The Novelist exits stage right. Some dancers sit on the stage while others stand around the front of the stage. Dorian realizes The Novelist has left and lurks behind the dancers to see what they're doing.

DANCER 1
What do Bloods eat when they're sick?

DANCER 2
... I don't know, man, what?

DANCER 1 *(in Blood call)*
Chicken Suwoop!

Dancers all cackle while Dorian decides they are harmless and starts to exit stage right.

DANCER 2

I got one! How many cops does it take to screw in a lightbulb?

DANCER 3

Doesn't matter. They just beat the room for being Black!

> *Dancers cackle again. Dorian*
> *slowly backs up on the stage*
> *and watches the dancers.*

DANCER 3

What do you tell a woman with two black eyes?

DANCER 1

Nothing—you already told her twice!

> *Dancers cackle again as*
> *Dorian runs up on them.*

DORIAN

What did you just say?

DANCER 2 *(surprised, then dismissive)*

Yo, chill, man, it's just a joke.

DORIAN

Is it still funny with a broken nose?

DANCER 1

You wanna do something?

DORIAN

I'm already doing it. Catch up.

DANCER 3

You about to catch these hands, son.

DORIAN

Like I'm scared of those hands.

> *Dancers jump on stage and start*
> *fighting with Dorian. Dorian*
> *lands a few good punches but then*
> *gets overwhelmed. Room fills with*
> *blue and red flashing lights and*
> *sirens, indicating police. Dancers*
> *scatter, leaving Dorian on the ground.*
> *He struggles to his feet and runs off stage*
> *into the audience and out the room.*

DANCER *(offstage or in audience)*

In America, more white people are killed in police shootings than Black people, but overall, white people are statistically *less likely* to be killed by police than Black people. Blue lives are choices. Black lives are birthrights.

> *Aisa enters from the back of the*
> *room. She remains in the aisle for the*
> *duration of the poem, though she*
> *paces toward and away from the stage.*

AISA

My mother dreams of fish before anyone announces
pregnancy in our family, but I always dream of knives.

Her fish hold optimism, swimmers on the verge
of evolutionary breakthrough. My knives glint fear, panic,
blades capable of permanent damage. But this is not about
vanity, elasticity, the countdown to a lover leaving.
Really—this is about the many ways a body can flee.
Knives come in all shapes, sizes, sharpness.
I've dreamed about them for three nights now,
and no one has announced. Maybe they aren't for new children
this time. Rather, they come when I'm about to go under,
to face my own slice and removal, just before
something vital or corrosive is to be extracted.

> *Aisa exits out the back of the*
> *room, wringing her hands. Fog rolls*
> *in. Opposite Aisa's exit, The Novelist*
> *enters at the back of the room*
> *with dancers, but they all stay back.*

THE NOVELIST
We learn to live in tragedy alongside beauty.
If my people did not laugh,
they would burn this world to the ground.

> *"The Cupid Shuffle" begins playing.*
> *House lights come on and the room*
> *floods with all the dancers and characters*
> *(except Dorian, Aisa, and Belle).*
> *They dance together, encouraging the*
> *audience to join them, dancing and*
> *singing along. Meanwhile, The Novelist*
> *moves through them and gets on stage.*
> *After a minute or two, the music*
> *fades, but the party can't end just yet.*

ALL *(singing)*
No music! *(clap, clap-clap, clap, clap)*
No music! *(clap, clap-clap, clap, clap)*
No music! *(clap, clap-clap, clap, clap)*
No music! *(clap, clap-clap, clap, clap)*

This continues for a few beats longer until The Novelist calls for them to stop by raising her hand. Everyone hushes and pauses. House lights go down. Everyone exits quietly, leaving The Novelist alone on stage. Aisa enters from stage right with a pregnancy test in her hand. She paces briefly, then checks her watch, and paces again. She checks her watch once more, then looks at the pregnancy test. Her face contorts as she realizes it's positive.

AISA *(to audience)*
Yay?

DANCER *(offstage or in audience)*
It's a myth that Black, Latinx, and Indigenous women do not have fertility problems. The assumption that women of color are "baby machines" comes from historical lack of access to birth control, marital and acquaintance rape, and patriarchal religious beliefs in unprotected marital sex.

Aisa reacts with annoyance to the interjection, then jumps when The Novelist addresses her, as this is the first time she's ever truly seen The Novelist.

THE NOVELIST
Aisa, the map that led you here
to this choice, with Dorian,
dictates you will have a son.
Do you want to keep the child?

AISA
What happens if I say no?

THE NOVELIST
You will still have a son. Later.
But you will never have another child.

AISA *(surprised)*
Never? Why?

> *The Novelist turns away from
> Aisa and says nothing. Aisa goes to ask
> her again when the dancer speaks.*

DANCER *(offstage or in audience)*
The U.S. has the highest maternal mortality rate of *all* developed countries.
(beat) About 26 out of every 100,000 pregnant women die each year.
Additionally, the CDC reports that Black women in the U.S. are three to
four times more likely to die from pregnancy-related causes as their white
counterparts.

> *Aisa hears the statistic but doesn't
> search for its source. She looks back
> at the pregnancy test, and then puts
> a hand on her belly, both thoughtful
> and deeply troubled. She looks to*

The Novelist, about to ask a
question, but then sighs heavily.

AISA *(looking at the pregnancy test)*
I didn't know they made maps this small.

Aisa fiddles with the test a beat
longer, then rushes off the stage toward
the back of the room and out the
doors. The Novelist watches her leave.
Dancers enter from the back of
the room and pair up, skipping/
playing like children through the aisles.

THE NOVELIST
How does the song go?

ALL DANCERS *(singing)*
Ring-around the rosie
A pocket full of posies
Ashes, ashes
We all fall down

Ring-around the rosie
A pocket full of posies
Ashes, ashes
All fall down

Ring-a-ring o' roses
A pocket full of posies
Achoo—achoo!
All fall down

Ring-a-ring o' roses
A pocket full of posies
(*coughing*) Achoo—achoo!
All fall down

> *Dancers stop skipping/playing*
> *and face audience, miming lyrics.*

ALL DANCERS (*singing*)
Hands above your head now
Don't resist arrest now
(*coughing*) Ashes, ashes
(*wheezing*) I—can't—breathe—

> *Dancers fall to their knees*
> *and clasp at their throats.*

ALL DANCERS (*singing*)
When it's all said and done
A good Black boy's a dead one
A good Black boy's a dead one
(*coughing/wheezing*) A good Black boy's a dead one
(*coughing/wheezing*) A good Black boy's a dead one ...

> *Dancers repeat the last line over*
> *and over while struggling to breathe.*
> *They all finally collapse on the floor,*
> *dead. After a beat of silence, The*
> *Novelist starts to hum the tune as*
> *she slowly crosses the stage. Once she*
> *finishes two verses, dancers stand*
> *and exit out the back of the room.*
> *Dorian enters stage right.*

DORIAN
Did you hear? I'm going to be a dad!

THE NOVELIST
Will you?

DORIAN
Yes! ... Wait. What do you know that I don't know?
(beat) Do I even *want* to know?

THE NOVELIST
That depends.
You have narrowly avoided the assumed fates of the Black man.
Do you want to see your future?

DORIAN
Is there only one road?

THE NOVELIST
There are always options.

> *The Novelist snaps. Ty and Luther*
> *enter, each wearing hoods/hats and*
> *black bandanas hiding their faces.*
> *A dancer enters and places a chair*
> *down centerstage. Dorian fades*
> *upstage, out of their way to watch.*

THE NOVELIST
Nature versus nurture, blessing or death sentence.
Now, colored child, let us see some good.

The Novelist walks behind Luther and taps them. Luther raises their head, and goes to sit down in the empty chair, removing their hood/hat and bandana. Five more dancers come on stage, some with chairs, and they exercise on the ground (pushups, crunches, yoga, etc.). Luther starts tapping their foot to start a metronome tempo. Song begins.

DANCER 1
My baby's waiting, waiting,

ALL
waiting on me on the outside.

DANCER 1
My baby's waiting, waiting,

ALL
waiting on me on the outside.
On the outside, on the outside.

DANCER 2 *(spoken off beat)*
Why you here?

LUTHER
Sold some grass.

DANCER 3
Paid for some ass.

DANCER 2
Shot up my class with an AK.

DANCER 5
Stole some cigs.

DANCER 1
Beat up my kids.

DANCER 4
Stabbed some bitch for his new J's.

ALL
Oh, Lord, please save my soul.
I promise I won't do this shit no more.

DANCER 3
Gotta get working, working,

ALL
working these hands on the outside.
On the outside, on the outside.

DANCER 4 *(spoken off beat)*
Why you back?

DANCER 3
Changed lanes too fast.

LUTHER
Kept selling grass.

DANCER 5
Lied 'bout my past to my GM.

DANCER 1
Violated parole.

DANCER 2
Oh hell, I don't know!

DANCER 5
Caught Mary Jo with my GM.

ALL
Oh, Lord, please save my soul.
I promise I won't do this shit no more.

DANCER 4
Can't keep living, living,

ALL
living this way on the outside.
On the outside, on the outside.

DANCER 2 *(spoken off beat)*
How long to go?

DANCER 3
'Bout 40 days.

DANCER 4
Till I see sun rays.

LUTHER
Just until May to see a rose bloom.

DANCER 5
A nickel and a dime.

DANCER 1
25 to life.

DANCER 2
They're gonna fry me in here soon.

ALL
Oh, Lord, please save my soul.
I promise I won't do this shit no more.

DANCER 2 *(slows down)*
I ain't never, never,
never gon' step foot on the outside.

ALL
On the outside, on the outside...

Luther and all but one dancer
exit stage right, taking chairs
and props with them.

DANCER *(just before exiting stage)*
There are more Black men incarcerated or under watch by the criminal
justice system today than were enslaved in 1850. African Americans make
up less than 15% of the population, but Black men make up over 40%
of prison inmates. Though people of color only account for 30% of the
American population, they account for 60% of those imprisoned.

Dancer exits. The Novelist
shakes her head.

THE NOVELIST
I *said*, show us some *good*, colored child.

The Novelist walks to Ty, stands behind
them, and taps their shoulder. They
stand up straight and walk downstage
to center. The Novelist fades upstage.
They lower their bandana and begin the
poem deep and slow, with the intensity
increasing as the poem progresses.

TY
When they find my body between drywall and insulation,
or my throat slit like a second smile, or my guts writhing
on ashy sidewalk, or my fingers digesting in the stomach
of some man, or my spine gunfire-curled, or my eyes

missing—when it is too late to ask why I was alone
or near water or not wearing a bulletproof vest or not studying
with my friends or not taking out the garbage or not home
watching sitcoms with my sister—do not ask who killed me.
Rather, dig into your own rotting cells. Ask what weapon
removes and loses children like me. Exhume the graves of my mothers.
Do not lay pennies at my fathers' feet, apologize into cameras, or
bury me with flowers. There is not enough gold to cover silence.
Not enough water to erode sin. I do not want your hash tags,
your legislature, your promises. No movement ever saved
melanin splattered on the city's walls. When they find me,
lit on a mountain signaling God to take us back—
(bellowing) do—not—pray.

> *Ty sits in the chair, takes off their hood/*
> *hat and bandana, and drops them on*
> *the floor. Two dancers enter stage left,*
> *cover Ty's head with a white sheet/*
> *pillowcase, and drag them struggling*
> *off stage right. A gun shot is heard*
> *followed by the thud of a body dropping.*

DANCER *(offstage or in audience)*
The leading cause of death for Black men ages 15 to 34 is homicide.

> *Beat. The Novelist floats down*
> *center stage and beckons Dorian.*
> *Still in shock of what he's seen,*
> *he slowly stumbles after her.*

DORIAN
That's the map you're offering?!
Locked up or murdered?
I can't prevent this at all?

THE NOVELIST
Of course, you can. It is your life, colored child.
Good is your destiny,
pleasure your birthright.

The Novelist exits. Dorian wrings
his hands, pacing around the
stage, his anger building.

DORIAN
I'm just supposed to be as good
as they want me to be. As beautiful
as will not threaten. As alive
as will not harm. I am only useful
for as long as they say so. At first—I built
"their" country on the bones and blood of the Natives,
absorbed a religion that glorified suffering, forgot
my own name. Over time, I lost my utility,
stopped being necessary. I couldn't be controlled
by chains, a whip, or a Bible. They called it freedom
but somehow, the scars on my back haven't healed.

There are a few acceptable types of Blackness, of manliness,
of being alive and being colored and being in your face.
They want me dead or locked up or talking enough
to justify either. Didn't Martin, Malcolm, and Medgar
talk too much? Am I talking too much for you?

Aisa enters at the back of the
room holding a swaddled child.

DANCER *(offstage or in audience)*
People of color are less likely to report domestic or sexual violence,
especially when perpetrated by men of color within their racial or ethnic

group, to protect their community from racist backlash and protect their perpetrators from a racist criminal justice system.

DANCER *(offstage or in audience)*
Black K-12 students are 3.8 times as likely to receive one or more out-of-school suspensions as white students.

DANCER *(offstage or in audience)*
Black people contract and die from COVID-19 at a rate three times higher than white people.

DANCER *(offstage or in audience)*
The folktale of John Henry encourages Black men to become pillars of their communities, literally working themselves to death to keep everyone alive by neglecting their personal health challenges.

DANCER *(offstage or in audience)*
Heart disease is the number one killer of Black individuals in the United States.

DANCER *(offstage or in audience)*
Black males represent the highest documented incidence and mortality rates for prostate cancers.

DANCER *(offstage or in audience)*
A Black child born today is less likely to be raised by both parents than a Black child born during slavery.

DORIAN
Stop! No more facts. No more stats. No more noise.

I've been looking for joy
in books and lovers and television
for as long as I've known how to laugh.
I won't stop being scared,
stop wondering if Blackness makes me
predisposed to violence, frailty, and loss. It does.
I know that now. The problem with politics is
you can't avoid them when your body is political.
I was born with this skin, this fire, this target
painted on my chest. How privileged to not get involved,
to go back to your lives and forget about this flesh
lying on the pavement, one more parent
who doesn't come home, one more funeral,
one more reason to send thoughts and prayers.

Don't send them. We can't use them.

Trauma is the fabric of America.
We love violence and call it human nature.
But I will not sacrifice my beloved
to fetishists of blood. Instead, I will raise a child
with clean hands, who learns what harm looks like
in the fingerprints of others. I want a new tradition
of pleasure in my children, reckless abandon in the name of beauty,
a map drawn in the pursuit of sustained disruption for justice.

Aisa approaches Dorian with
their child, and Dorian takes
the baby in his arms.

DORIAN *(looking at the baby)*
All I ever wanted was to live long enough
to raise someone better than me, someone
I could hold with clean hands,
who knows their way home.

I want them to remember how much I loved them,
the reverberation of my laugh.

AISA *(smiling)*
Like a song stuck in your head.

> *Sudden music plays. Stage and audience
> flood with all performers, alive and dead,
> who dance. They bring audience members
> on stage and into the aisles to dance with
> them. It feels like a reunion of lost and
> loved ones, as if no one has ever been
> hurt, scared, or brokenhearted. Dorian's
> family embraces one another, so grateful
> to be together again. The celebration goes
> on for about the length of a song until the
> music ends abruptly. At its end, Dorian
> stands on a chair at the front of the room
> but not on stage. Belle, Neil, Raven, and
> Aisa, holding the baby, stand around
> him. Dancers all stop and look toward
> him. They appear relieved and grateful
> to be together. Neil holds hands with
> Raven and kisses his mother on the cheek.
> Dorian smiles wide, taking the baby from
> Aisa. Fog rolls in slowly, but with the
> lights on, no one notices at first.*

DORIAN
Really, all I want to be is a good ancestor.

> *Belle, Raven, Neil, and Aisa echo
> Dorian's line, staggered.*

BELLE
A good ancestor.

        RAVEN
        A good ancestor.

                NEIL
                A good ancestor.

                        AISA
                        A good ancestor.

ALL DANCERS
A good ancestor.

                  The Novelist enters from stage
                  right and goes to Dorian as
                  he speaks. Fog intensifies.

DORIAN
When you build your altar, with my face
surrounded by candles and offerings—
say my name as prayer.

                            Beat.

THE NOVELIST *(to Dorian)*
Look at the map you drew, colored child.
You did good. Very good.

*The Novelist extends her hand to
Dorian. He takes her hand and steps off
the chair. The Novelist releases him and
starts to walk out the back of the room.
Dorian gives the child to Belle, and
follows The Novelist out, shaking hands
and saying hello and thanking everyone
he meets. Once they both leave the room,
a gunshot is heard. Neil, Raven, and
Aisa sprint after Dorian out the back of
the room, screaming his name. Dancers
exit. Belle soothes the baby and speaks
once the commotion simmers.*

BELLE *(to the baby)*
You deserve to grow old, colored child.
You deserve to grow old.

*Belle exits with the baby,
leaving audience members in the
aisles and on stage. Lights out.*

ACKNOWLEDGEMENTS

Thank you doesn't even begin to encompass my gratitude. But I'll try to articulate it anyway.

To my editor, Andrew Gifford, who didn't know what this was but knew it was worthy of publication; to Christopher Romaguera, who served as a reader and editor near the end of this process and gave me the much needed support to push this book to the finish line; and to the whole SFWP team—our social media team, my managing editor Nicole Schmidt, and all my press mates—thank you for championing this project.

To Robert Barkley—this is the choreopoem that made you fall in love with me. I love you eternally. 1sw34rmyf34lty.

To my family, and especially Celeste Prince who introduced me to Ntozake Shange's work in the first place—thank you for always loving me, letting me be myself, and staying proud of me.

To Jessica Fischoff for publishing *How to Exterminate the Black Woman*, where the character of Dorian first hit the stage—you are a queen and a gem.

To Adam al-Sirgany—Dorian is ours. Thank you for loving me through this.

To my polycule—oh, how I love you all so.

To my original cast and crew of *Roadmap* at Susquehanna University in 2019—can you even believe this weird show you did in between the rest of your responsibilities is now a published book?! You believed in my work simply because you believed in me. I cannot repay you—but you will have recommendation letters from me for life. I promised I will always take care of you; thanks for not making me a liar.

To Ntozake Shange, the original creator of the choreopoem—I am because you were. To Anya Pearson, Bryan-Keyth Wilson, and all the others working in this genre—thank you for continuing the choreopoem's legacy with me.

To my Selinsgrove community of color—especially Danielle Brown, Sharief Hashim, Shannon Musgrove, Aisha Upton, Rachel Rockwell, and Stacey Pearson-Wharton—thank you for reading earlier drafts of this in my living room, giving me feedback, and holding it down for us in this little town we've chosen.

To my literary community—including but not limited to Barrelhouse, [PANK], Cricket Hill Writing Residency, *Another Chicago Magazine*, *The Rumpus*, *The Texas Review*, *Madcap Review*, Readings on the Pike, Alan Squire Publishing, The 5th Woman, *The Fourth River*, Chatham University, Tire Fire, Exhibit B, The Writer's Center, Whiskey Tit, Tupelo Press, *American Poetry Journal*, the Susquehanna University English & Creative Writing and Theatre departments, and so many others who read pieces of this manuscript, gave me money/time/space to work on it, or supported me through readings, promotion, and cheerleading—thank you for letting me say yes, say no, and ask for more.

To the original Dorian, my only colored child—this is for you. Rest well.

PRODUCTION HISTORY

Roadmap received its first full-length production at Susquehanna University in Selinsgrove, PA on April 13-14, 2019. It was directed by Monica Prince, stage managed by Jasmine Tarver, and choreographed by Ashley Ward. Lights, sound, and props were provided by Monica Prince, Jasmine Tarver, and the Susquehanna University Department of Theatre.

THE NOVELIST . . . . PRECIOUS EMMANUEL

DORIAN . . . . DEVEN DANCY

BELLE . . . . HANIFAH JONES

RAVEN . . . . TOLULOPE ILORI

NEIL . . . . SAMUEL EMMANUEL

AISA . . . . BIANCA MOFFITT

TY . . . . JAHMIR WILSON

NOELLE . . . . EMILY LUA-LUA

LUTHER . . . . SAMSON WHEELER

DANCERS . . . . ISRAEL COLLAZO-LUCIANO

KARA LITTLE

ANTHONY McCOY

TAY MEEHAN

ANDREA REPETZ

ANTHONY ZAMOT

STAGE CREW . . . . EM CURTIS

LIA TAYLOR

ASHLEIGH TOMCICS

PRODUCTION NOTES

The author requires the director to cast this choreopoem accurately. See dramatis personae for more specific information about color-conscious casting opportunities.

The choreopoem can be performed in a theater-in-the round setting, or on a traditional stage space, provided performers have access to the audience from backstage. Fog can be substituted for lights. Even though "Cloudless Afternoon" calls for ten dancers, as many dancers can repeat the lines as are available.

NOTES

The names called out during "A Child, A Shot, A Name" refer to Trayvon Martin, Antwon Rose II, and Tamir Rice. Rest in power, young ones.

In "Roadmap: Family Tree," the line "an island behind God's back" refers to Paule Marshall's novels, *Brown Girl, Brownstones* and *The Chosen Place, The Timeless People*.

"Cut" is a half-Pecha Kucha based on the photography exhibit *Historical Fiction* by Tyler Shields. The line "if we are all refugees of our childhoods" is a paraphrase of a quote by Mohsin Hamid: "We are all refugees of our childhood because we can never return to that place."

In "Tongues and Tattoos," the line "we drown in the sticky parts" is a reference to Matthew Dickman's poem, "Love."

In "Expectations," the line "A woman should praise the man—the king" is a quote from DJ Khaled.

The quote in "Call It Love" comes from Nikki Giovanni's poem, "Nikki-Rosa."

"Expectations" and "Call It Love" appear in a slightly different version in *Black Visions: A Jeffrey "Boosie" Bolden Anthology* by The Fourth River, published in May 2022.

"Attention is the most basic form of love" is attributed to John Tarrant.

"Beautiful things deserve beautiful things" is a quote within the television show, *Good Behavior*, season 1, episode 5.

In "Nursery Rhyme: for Eric Garner," the first two verses are the American version of "Ring Around the Rosie," and the second two verses are the British version of the same nursery rhyme. The line "a good Black boy is a dead one" comes from Sonya Renee Taylor's poem, "When the Shotgun Questions the Black Boy's Heart." Rest in power, Eric Garner.

"Do Not Pray" originally appeared in *American Poetry Journal*, Issue 18.2, July 2020.

In "Past, Present, Prophecy," the line "Didn't Martin, Malcom, and Medgar / talk too much?" references civil rights activists Rev. Dr. Martin Luther King, Jr., Malcolm (Little) X, and Medgar Evans of the American Civil Rights Movement during the 1950s and 1960s. The line "of being alive and being colored and being in your face" is a reconstruction of Ntozake Shange's line "bein alive and bein a woman and bein colored" from "no more love poems #4" in *For colored girls who have considered suicide / when the rainbow is enuf* (1975).

The reconstruction of the line "I want to be a good ancestor" is attributed to Layla Saad.

All statistics, quotes, and paraphrases recited by dancers during and between poems, as well as research that informed the poems "Call It Love," "Different," "Black Boys are Missing," and "On the Outside," come from the sources listed below. When performing, producers and dramaturgs cannot update these lines, but rather encourage audience conversation if these facts change after publication.

Alexander, Michelle. *The New Jim Crow: Mass Incarceration in the Age of Colorblindness*. The New Press: New York, 2010.

Barksdale, Crystal L., PhD, MPH, Rhonda C. Boyd, PhD, and Ellyson Stout, MS. "Preventing Suicide and Self-harm among Black Youth." *Preventing Suicide and Self-Harm Among Black Youth | Children's Safety Network*. Children's Safety Network, 10 Sept. 2020. Web. Retrieved 23 Sept. 2021.

Beard, Jennifer, Godfrey Biemba, Mohamad I. Brooks, Jill Costello, Mark Ommerborn, Megan Bresnahan, David Flynn, and Jonathon L. Simon. "Children of Female Sex Workers and Drug Users: A Review of Vulnerability, Resilience and Family-centered Models of Care." *Journal of the International AIDS Society*. The International AIDS Society, n.d. Web. 15 Aug. 2015.

Blanco, Janell. "Prison Violence: Types, Causes & Statistics." *Study.com*. N.p., 2015. Web. 13 Oct. 2015.

Bureau of Prisons. "BOP Statistics: Inmate Offenses." *Federal Bureau of Prisons*. N.p., 26 Sept. 2015. Web. 13 Oct. 2015.

Campbell, Alexia Fernández. "Five Myths About Women of Color, Infertility, and IVF Debunked." *The Atlantic*, Atlantic Media Company, 3 Sept. 2015. Web. 28 Jan. 2019.

"CDC: Black Women Murdered by Domestic Partners More than Women of Any Other Race." *Blavity News & Politics*, Blavity, 21 July 2017. Web. 26 Sept. 2021.

Domestic Violence Roundtable. "Effects of Domestic Violence on Children." *Effects of Domestic Violence on Children*. N.p., 2008. Web. 20 Aug. 2015.

Emery, C. Eugene, Jr. "Does Becoming a Prostitute Mean You've Only Got about 7 Years to Live?" *@politifact*. N.p., 31 May 2015. Web. 15 Aug. 2015.

Green, Tahirah Alexander. "Black People Self Harm, Too." *The Black Youth Project*. The Black Youth Project, 30 Nov. 2019. Web. 23 Sept. 2021.

"Health Equity: Leading Causes of Death in Males, 2015." *Centers for Disease Control and Prevention*. Centers for Disease Control and Prevention, 16 Apr. 2018. Web. 17 July 2018.

Holmes, Lindsay. "10 Staggering Stats on How Mental Health Care Fails People of Color." *The Huffington Post*. TheHuffingtonPost.com, 19 Aug. 2016. Web. 17 July 2018.

Johnson, Akilah, and Nina Martin. "How Covid 19 Hollowed out a Generation of Young Black Men." *ProPublica*. ProPublica, 22 Dec. 2020. Web. 22 Dec. 2020.

Kerby, Sophia. "The Top 10 Most Startling Facts About People of Color and Criminal Justice in the United States." *Center for American Progress*. N.p., 29 May 2015. Web. 17 July 2018.

"Marriage in Black America." *BlackDemographics.com*. N.p., n.d. Web. 17 July 2018.

"More Black Men Are in Prison Today Than Were Slaves In 1850, Law Professor Says." *The Huffington Post*. TheHuffingtonPost.com, 13 Oct. 2011. Web. 17 July 2018.

O, Amanda. "Everyone's Missing the Obvious About the Declining U.S. Birth Rate." *Medium.com*, Medium, 27 Jan. 2019. Web. 31 Jan. 2019.

Palma, Bethania. "FACT CHECK: Do Police Kill More White People Than Black People?" *Snopes.com*, 26 Sept. 2017. Web. 9 Aug. 2018.

Sered, Danielle. *Young Men of Color and the Other Side of Harm: Addressing Disparities in Our Responses to Violence*. New York: Vera Institute of Justice, 2015.

"Silence Strengthens Impact of Depression Among Men." *Tell Me More* from NPR, 8 Sept. 2008, https://www.npr.org/templates/transcript/transcript.php?storyId=94379107. Retrieved 28 September 2021.

Simeron, Alexa-Jade. "Health Conditions That Disproportionately Affect Black Americans." *Health & Wellness*. Summit Health, 01 Feb. 2021. Web. 26 Sept. 2021.

The Mask You Live In. Directed by Jennifer Siebel Newsom, performance by Ashanti Branch, Caroline Heldman, Michael Kimmel, and Dr. Joseph Marshall. Arts Alliance America, 2015. *YouTube*, https://www.youtube.com/watch?v=ErOHoTHBf7Q. Retrieved 30 September 2021.

Toppo, Greg. "Black Students Nearly 4x as Likely to Be Suspended." *USA Today*, Gannett Satellite Information Network, 7 June 2016. 12 Aug. 2018.

Triffin, Molly. "If They Cheated Once, Will They Cheat Again?" *Women's Health*. Women's Health, 25 May 2018. Web. 17 July 2018.

ABOUT THE AUTHOR

Monica Prince teaches activist and performance writing at Susquehanna University. Her books include *How to Exterminate the Black Woman: A Choreopoem*, *Instructions for Temporary Survival*, and *Letters from the Other Woman*. Born to Guyanese parents and obsessed with maxi skirts with pockets, she writes, teaches, directs, and performs choreopoems all over the country, but is mostly found on Twitter @poetic_moni or on her website, monicaprince.com.